THE STORY OF
CIVILIZATION

VOLUME III
THE MAKING OF THE MODERN WORLD

TEST BOOK

ISBN: 978-1-5051-0985-6

Published in the United States by
TAN Books
P.O. Box 410487
Charlotte, NC 28241
www.TANBooks.com

Printed in the United States of America

THE STORY OF CIVILIZATION

VOLUME III
THE MAKING OF THE MODERN WORLD

From the Reformation
to the Twenty-First Century

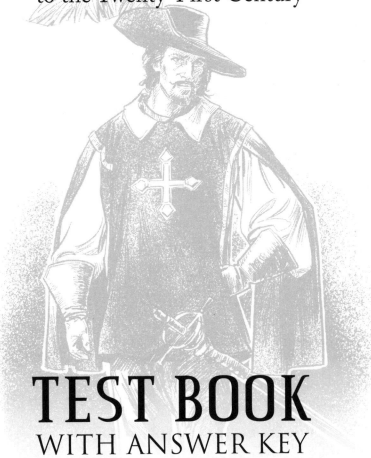

TEST BOOK
WITH ANSWER KEY

CONTENTS

CHAPTER 1
The Glory of the Renaissance

Perfect Score: 100   Your Score: _____

Multiple Choice

Directions: For each numbered item, circle the letter beside the choice (A, B, C, or D) that best answers the question or completes the statement. Circle only one choice per item. Each correct answer is worth 5 points. 50 possible points.

1. The word *Renaissance* means:

A. Christendom.
B. rebirth.
C. piety.
D. patronage.

2. One thing the Renaissance is famous for is its:

A. wars.
B. powerful kings.
C. art.
D. technology.

3. Often wealthy or influential people would pay famous artists to decorate their cities. This was known as:

A. patronage.
B. competition.
C. restoration.
D. mannerism.

4. The invention of this device meant more people could read than ever before.

A. printing press
B. compass
C. mechanical clock
D. gunpowder

5. These two cities competed to become the artistic capital of Italy.

A. Florence and Venice
B. Rome and Venice
C. Pisa and Florence
D. Florence and Rome

6. Jan van Eyck, Pieter Bruegel, and Hieronymus Bosch were _____ painters.

A. Florentine
B. Dutch and Flemish
C. English
D. Venetian

7. Besides religious works, the Dutch and Flemish masters liked to paint scenes of:

A. warfare.
B. royalty.
C. skeletons dancing.
D. common life.

8. The famous painting the *Arnolfini Marriage* was painted by:

A. Donatello.
B. Brunelleschi.
C. Pieter Bruegel.
D. Jan van Eyck.

9. People of the Renaissance enjoyed drawing inspiration from the stories of:

A. ancient Babylon.
B. the discoveries of the New World.
C. ancient Greece and Rome.
D. Dutch and French common life.

10. Many of the most notable artists of the Renaissance were:

A. Italian.
B. English.
C. Spanish.
D. Polish.

True or False?

Directions: In the blank beside each statement, write "T" if the statement is *True* or "F" if the statement is *False*. Each correct answer is worth 5 points. 50 possible points.

_____ 1. The popes were great patrons of Renaissance art.

_____ 2. Renaissance artists often competed with each other.

_____ 3. The sculptors Brunelleschi and Donatello were bitter enemies.

_____ 4. In the famous competition between Brunelleschi and Donatello, Donatello admitted that Brunelleschi's crucifix was better.

_____ 5. Christians of the Renaissance generally did not think the Church was in need of reform.

_____ 6. The Renaissance was a great time of art and Catholic piety.

_____ 7. Michelangelo, Botticelli, Donatello, Brunelleschi, Raphael, and Leonardo da Vinci were all artists who worked for the Medici in Florence.

_____ 8. Michelangelo and da Vinci were great friends and were able to work together to complete a fresco for the city of Florence.

_____ 9. The Dutch and Flemish come from the regions of Holland and Flanders.

_____ 10. The Dutch and Flemish artists were famous for their portraits.

CHAPTER 2
Columbus and the New World

Perfect Score: 100   Your Score: _____

Matching

Directions: In each blank beside a phrase, write the letter of the term that is described by that phrase. Each item is worth 10 points. 100 possible points.

A. China
B. Portugal
C. Genoa
D. East
E. West

F. Spain
G. Reconquista
H. *Niña*, *Pinta*, and *Santa María*
I. San Salvador
J. Taíno

_____ 1. Christopher Columbus came from this Italian city.

_____ 2. A centuries-long struggle of the Spanish Christians to retake their lands from the Muslim Moors.

_____ 3. The name Columbus gave to the island he "discovered."

_____ 4. Columbus believed you could get to China by sailing in this direction.

_____ 5. Throughout the Middle Ages, Europeans were very interested in finding the best route here.

_____ 6. The three ships of Christopher Columbus.

_____ 7. This kingdom had discovered a sea route to India by going south around Africa.

_____ 8. The sea route to China going this direction took far too long.

_____ 9. Ferdinand and Isabella were king and queen of _____.

_____ 10. The natives Columbus met in the new world were known as the _____.

CHAPTER 3
Martin Luther

Perfect Score: 100   Your Score: _____

True or False?

Directions: In the blank beside each statement, write "T" if the statement is *True* or "F" if the statement is *False*. Each correct answer is worth 5 points. 100 possible points.

_____ 1. In the late Middle Ages, parish priests were sometimes not as well educated as they should have been.

_____ 2. An indulgence is a mitigation or lessening of penance for sins already confessed.

_____ 3. Since Christ promised the Church would always endure, that means no leader in the Church will ever make a bad decision.

_____ 4. Martin Luther was excommunicated by the pope.

_____ 5. To recant something means to take it back.

_____ 6. Martin Luther was a Franciscan monk.

_____ 7. When reading the Bible, Luther believed people should follow the interpretation of the Catholic Church's tradition.

_____ 8. Martin Luther believed the popes and councils had taught wrong things.

_____ 9. Martin Luther believed in the power and effectiveness of indulgences.

_____ 10. Bishop Albert of Brandenburg was lying to the Catholics of his diocese to get money.

_____ 11. *Simony* means the buying or selling of spiritual things.

_____ 12. Even popes and priests need God's grace.

_____ 13. Even though he disagreed with the pope, Luther believed the pope was a good Christian man.

_____ 14. The Edict of Worms forbade anyone from helping Luther and called for his capture.

_____ 15. When Martin Luther saw that the pope had excommunicated him, he repented of his heresy and returned to the Church.

_____ 16. The papal theologian sent to challenge Martin Luther was Johann Eck.

_____ 17. Martin Luther believed that people did not need to do penance for their sins.

_____ 18. The _95 Theses_ were written by Pope Leo X.

_____ 19. Luther defended his teachings before Emperor Charles V.

_____ 20. _Scandal_ means losing faith because of somebody else's sins.

CHAPTER 4
Germany on Fire

Perfect Score: 100   Your Score: _____

Multiple Choice

Directions: For each numbered item, circle the letter beside the choice (A, B, C, or D) that best answers the question or completes the statement. Circle only one choice per item. Each correct answer is worth 10 points. 100 possible points.

1. Many nobles and knights joined Luther's movement because they wanted to take the Church's:

A. money.
B. reputation.
C. lands.
D. art.

2. Some people did not want the pope meddling in German affairs because he was:

A. too mean.
B. saintly.
C. wealthy.
D. not a German.

3. This man led an attack against the city of Frankenhausen, attempting to overthrow the bishops and nobles.

A. Martin Luther
B. Johann Eck
C. Thomas Müntzer
D. Ludwig of Weinsberg

4. Count Ludwig of Weinsberg was murdered by:

A. the peasants.
B. his nobles.
C. the Holy Roman emperor.
D. Martin Luther.

5. When Martin Luther heard about the revolt of the peasants, he was:

A. very happy with them.
B. hoping it would cause the downfall of the Holy Roman Empire.
C. blaming himself for the disaster.
D. angry with the peasants and thought they should be killed.

6. After many years of fighting, Emperor Charles V told the princes of his empire that:

A. everybody had to embrace Lutheranism.
B. everybody had to return to Catholicism.
C. every prince could choose whatever religion he wanted for his kingdom.
D. everyone should just throw up their hands and become Muslim.

7. When peace had been attained, Charles V:

A. went out to battle one last time against the Lutherans.
B. gave up the throne and went into a monastery.
C. went on a pilgrimage to Rome.
D. threw a lavish party.

8. The first kingdom in Christendom to be split by the new heresies was:

A. the Holy Roman Empire.
B. France.
C. England.
D. Italy.

9. This group of people took Luther's preaching about freedom to mean that they did not need to obey the nobles.

A. clergy
B. peasants
C. lawyers
D. monks

10. The peasant revolt ended when:

A. the peasants successfully overthrew the empire.
B. Martin Luther was able to make peace between the peasants and their lords.
C. the peasants had to go home for the harvest.
D. the nobles slaughtered the peasant armies.

CHAPTER 5
Henry VIII and Anglicanism

Perfect Score: 100   Your Score: _____

Matching

Directions: In each blank beside a phrase, write the letter of the term that is described by that phrase. Each item is worth 5 points. 50 possible points.

A. Protestants
B. Tudor
C. annulment
D. Defender of the Faith
E. Arthur
F. England
G. Eucharist
H. St. John Fisher
I. Henry VIII
J. Pope Clement VII

_____ 1. King who broke England away from the Catholic Church.

_____ 2. This name originally referred to those who protested against Charles V's efforts to keep his empire Catholic.

_____ 3. A decree by the Church that a marriage never existed.

_____ 4. Henry VIII was king of this kingdom.

_____ 5. This pope refused to grant King Henry VIII his annulment.

_____ 6. This title was once granted by the pope to King Henry VIII.

_____ 7. The royal family of King Henry VII and Henry VIII.

_____ 8. All Protestants denied that this was the physical Body and Blood of Jesus Christ.

_____ 9. First husband of Catherine of Aragon who died young.

_____ 10. Bishop of Rochester, executed by Henry VIII.

Multiple Choice

Directions: For each numbered item, circle the letter beside the choice (A, B, C, or D) that best answers the question or completes the statement. Circle only one choice per item. Each correct answer is worth 5 points. 50 possible points.

1. Catherine of Aragon was the daughter of:

A. Henry VII and Queen Margaret.
B. Ferdinand and Isabella of Spain.
C. Henry VIII and Anne Boleyn.
D. Prince Arthur and Anne Boleyn.

2. This man was once chancellor of England but was later executed by Henry VIII for refusing to say that Henry was the head of the Church.

A. John Fisher
B. Richard Rich
C. William Warham
D. Thomas More

3. After he got rid of his first wife, King Henry VIII married this woman.

A. Anne Boleyn
B. Catherine of Aragon
C. Isabella of Castile
D. Mary Tudor

4. Bishop John Fisher made Henry VIII angry because he:

A. attacked Martin Luther.
B. disbelieved in the Eucharist.
C. defended Queen Catherine.
D. said Henry was a fat, pompous slob.

5. Anne Boleyn was a:

A. Catholic.
B. Jew.
C. Protestant.
D. German.

6. The name of the new church established by King Henry was the:

A. Lutheran Church.
B. Presbyterian Church.
C. Church of Scotland.
D. Anglican Church.

7. Henry gave orders that:

A. his religious followers could not communicate with Rome.
B. laws be passed to make clergy entirely dependent on him.
C. Catholic bishops be replaced with men sympathetic to Protestantism.
D. all of the above.

8. King Henry forced every cleric and royal official to:

A. swear an oath that the king was the supreme head of the Church in England.
B. give him ten pounds of gold.
C. resign from their posts.
D. wear ridiculous green tights.

9. Henry believed that it was wrong for him to have:

A. closed the monasteries.
B. argued with the pope.
C. married his brother's widow.
D. attacked Luther.

10. The daughter of King Henry and Queen Catherine was:

A. Anne.
B. Mary.
C. Elizabeth.
D. Isabella.

CHAPTER 6
The French Wars of Religion

Perfect Score: 100　　　　　　　　　　　　　　　Your Score: _____

True or False?

Directions: In the blank beside each statement, write "T" if the statement is *True* or "F" if the statement is *False*. Each correct answer is worth 5 points. 50 possible points.

_____ 1. Protestants covered the city of Paris with posters attacking the Mass.

_____ 2. King Francis I supported the Protestants and encouraged them to spread their teaching in France.

_____ 3. Churches organized on the model proposed by John Calvin are called Presbyterian.

_____ 4. King Henri II was accidentally killed in a jousting tournament.

_____ 5. Calvin was very unpopular in France.

_____ 6. Catherine de' Medici was the queen of France.

_____ 7. The Guises were a Protestant family, and the Bourbons were a Catholic family.

_____ 8. Henry of Navarre converted to Catholicism in order to be accepted by the people of Paris.

_____ 9. King Henry IV refused to allow Huguenots freedom of worship.

_____ 10. Future French kings were very happy with the Edict of Nantes.

Multiple Choice

Directions: For each numbered item, circle the letter beside the choice (A, B, C, or D) that best answers the question or completes the statement. Circle only one choice per item. Each correct answer is worth 5 points. 50 possible points.

1. John Calvin's book was called:

A. *The Freedom of the Christian.*
B. *The Institutes of the Christian Religion.*
C. *Against the Robbing and Murdering Hordes of Peasants.*
D. *Presbyterianism Made Easy.*

2. The Calvinist belief that God chooses for all eternity who will go to heaven and who will go to hell without taking into account anything they do is known as:

A. Predestination.
B. Presbyterianism.
C. Huguenotism.
D. Orthodoxy.

3. The wars between the Guises and the Bourbons were known as the:

A. Peasants' War.
B. War of the Schmalkaldic League.
C. French Wars of Religion.
D. Wars of the Roses.

4. Which of the following was *not* one of Calvin's teachings?

A. Mankind is totally and absolutely evil.
B. God decides for all eternity who will go to heaven or hell.
C. People who are once saved may lose their salvation.
D. The Church should not have bishops.

5. After he left France, John Calvin became the leader of the city of:

A. Paris.
B. Geneva.
C. Rome.
D. Versailles.

6. French Calvinists were called:

A. Huguenots.
B. Anglicans.
C. Presbyterians.
D. Lutherans.

7. What did the Edict of Nantes do?

A. exiled Huguenots from France
B. proclaimed Calvinism the official religion of France
C. forbid Huguenots from carrying weapons
D. gave Huguenots freedom of religion and one hundred fortified cities

8. King Henry IV was originally known as:

A. Henry Bourbon of Navarre.
B. Henri II.
C. Henry VIII.
D. Henry VII.

9. Sir Gabriel Montgomery killed:

A. the Duke of Guise.
B. King Henri II.
C. King Henry IV.
D. Catherine de' Medici.

10. Presbyterianism is the idea that the Church should have:

A. no dancing.
B. no stained-glass windows.
C. three-hour sermons.
D. no authority above the parish level.

CHAPTER 7
Mary, Queen of Scots

Perfect Score: 100   Your Score: _____

Multiple Choice

Directions: For each numbered item, circle the letter beside the choice (A, B, C, or D) that best answers the question or completes the statement. Circle only one choice per item. Each correct answer is worth 10 points. 100 possible points.

1. For protection, Scotland made an alliance with:

A. England.
B. Germany.
C. France.
D. Ireland.

2. The father of Mary, Queen of Scots, was:

A. King James V.
B. King Henry VIII.
C. King Francis II.
D. John Knox.

3. John Knox was a Protestant reformer who followed the teachings of:

A. Martin Luther.
B. John Calvin.
C. the Anglican Church.
D. Ulrich Zwingli.

4. The "Lords of the Congregation" were:

A. a group of Catholic nobles who opposed John Knox.
B. the Scottish lords who supported Queen Mary.
C. a group of Protestant lords who supported Knox and wanted the Church's lands.
D. a code name for the Scottish Jesuits.

5. The Lords of the Congregation warned Queen Mary that she should not:

A. attend Mass in public.
B. convert to Calvinism.
C. get married.
D. seek the throne of England.

6. John Knox believed that women:

A. made the best monarchs.
B. should not be allowed to rule.
C. were from the devil.
D. should be excommunicated.

7. After she came to Scotland, Queen Mary married and had a son with:

A. the earl of Moray.
B. James V.
C. Lord Darnley.
D. Lord Bothwell.

8. The Lords of the Congregation defeated Mary and this man, who was her last husband.

A. Lord Darnley
B. Lord Bothwell
C. The earl of Moray
D. James V

9. Queen Mary fled Scotland and sought help from her cousin:

A. Anne Boleyn.
B. Mary Tudor.
C. the earl of Moray.
D. Elizabeth.

10. Queen Elizabeth thought Mary was a threat to her throne and:

A. exiled her to France.
B. forced her to abdicate the throne of Scotland.
C. had her beheaded.
D. forced her to marry an English lord.

CHAPTER 8
The Counter-Reformation

Perfect Score: 100   Your Score: _____

Matching

Directions: In each blank beside a phrase, write the letter of the term that is described by that phrase. Each item is worth 5 points. 50 possible points.

A. Pope Paul III
B. Ecumenical Council
C. Council of Trent
D. seminaries

E. Counter-Reformation
   (Catholic Reformation)
F. St. Charles Borromeo
G. St. Ignatius Loyola

H. St. Francis Xavier
J. St. Peter Canisius
I. Jesuits

_____ 1. When bishops from the entire Church, in union with the pope, gather to discuss matters of doctrine and discipline.

_____ 2. He founded the first seminaries in the diocese of Milan.

_____ 3. It lasted from 1545 to 1563 and reaffirmed many traditional Catholic teachings.

_____ 4. The movement of spirituality and art that followed the Council of Trent.

_____ 5. This man summoned the Council of Trent.

_____ 6. This Spanish saint founded the Society of Jesus, also known as the Jesuits.

_____ 7. Schools for training priests.

_____ 8. He founded colleges all over Europe to bring Protestants back to the faith.

_____ 9. Traveled as a missionary to India and East Asia.

_____ 10. An order of priests dedicated to education, missionary work, and the spiritual formation of young people.

Multiple Choice

Directions: For each numbered item, circle the letter beside the choice (A, B, C, or D) that best answers the question or completes the statement. Circle only one choice per item. Each correct answer is worth 5 points. 50 possible points.

1. Ecumenical councils are often summoned in times when:

A. destructive heresies are confusing the Christian people.
B. everything is perfect and there's no trouble in the world.
C. the pope is confused about what to do.
D. Rome has been conquered by a foreign army.

2. Which one of the following was *not* one of the purposes of the Council of Trent?

A. to clarify Church teaching on things the Protestants attacked
B. to reform the life and morals of the clergy
C. to encourage priests, bishops, and the religious to be holier and set better examples for their people
D. to condemn the heresy of Arianism

3. The Council of Trent was:

A. held without interruption from 1545 to 1549.
B. was sometimes interrupted by wars or other problems.
C. attended by all the monarchs of Christendom.
D. summoned by Pope Leo X.

4. Which of the following was not a teaching of the Council of Trent?

A. Catholics get their faith from the Bible and Tradition
B. Faith, hope, and charity are necessary to get to heaven
C. The veneration of saints and the use of images in worship are bad
D. The Body and Blood of Christ are truly present in the Blessed Sacrament

5. The Council of Trent commanded bishops to:

A. be in charge of at least two dioceses at once.
B. live in their dioceses.
C. live in Rome.
D. live in the court of the king of whatever kingdom they were from.

6. One result of the Council of Trent was that:

A. artists created many works of religious art to promote the teachings of the council.
B. Priests and the religious dedicated themselves to God with renewed piety.
C. the Catholic Church was reformed.
D. all of the above.

7. St. Charles Borromeo is the patron saint of:

A. parish priests.
B. popes.
C. bishops.
D. people wounded by gunfire.

8. Besides seminaries, St. Charles Borromeo is known for founding:

A. the Jesuit order.
B. the first Sunday school for children.
C. the missions of China and India.
D. Knights of Columbus pancake breakfasts.

9. This Spanish saint originally wanted to be a knight until he was wounded by a cannonball.

A. St. Ignatius Loyola
B. St. Vincent Ferrer
C. St. Peter Canisius
D. St. Charles Borromeo

10. These men took a special vow of obedience to the pope.

A. Lutherans
B. seminarians
C. Jesuits
D. Turks

CHAPTER 9
Pope St. Pius V and the Battle of Lepanto

Perfect Score: 100   Your Score: _____

True or False?

Directions: In the blank beside each statement, write "T" if the statement is *True* or "F" if the statement is *False*. Each correct answer is worth 10 points. 100 possible points.

_____ 1. Contemplative religious orders spend all their time out in the world working or doing other activities.

_____ 2. St. Teresa of Avila believed that Carmelite nuns should be focused more on their spiritual lives.

_____ 3. St. John of the Cross was once locked up and whipped by some monks who did not approve of his reforms.

_____ 4. The Christians of Cyprus were able to successfully defeat their Turkish invaders.

_____ 5. The Christian alliance that went to fight the Turks was called the Holy League.

_____ 6. Pope Pius V personally led the ships of the Holy League into battle.

_____ 7. The Turkish ships at Lepanto were rowed by Christian slaves.

_____ 8. The Christian ships of the Holy League were rowed by Muslims slaves.

_____ 9. The Christian victory at Lepanto devastated the Turkish fleet and stopped the westward conquests of the Ottomans for more than a century.

_____ 10. John of Austria commanded the Christian ships at Lepanto.

CHAPTER 10
The Age of Elizabeth

Perfect Score: 100   Your Score: _____

Multiple Choice

Directions: For each numbered item, circle the letter beside the choice (A, B, C, or D) that best answers the question or completes the statement. Circle only one choice per item. Each correct answer is worth 5 points. 50 possible points.

1. After the death of Henry VIII, his very young son took the throne. His son's name was:

A. Henry IX.
B. Edward VI.
C. Thomas Wyatt.
D. James VI.

2. Mary Tudor was the daughter of Henry VIII by his wife:

A. Catherine of Aragon.
B. Elizabeth.
C. Anne Boleyn.
D. Mary Stuart.

3. Some English nobles did not like that Mary wanted to get married to a:

A. Lutheran.
B. Italian prince.
C. Spanish prince.
D. dwarf.

4. Sir Thomas Wyatt and his rebels demanded that:

A. the Catholic faith be restored in England.
B. King Edward VI end the Penal Laws.
C. Pius V excommunicate Elizabeth.
D. Queen Mary be removed and replaced with her half sister, Elizabeth.

5. This Protestant leader was burned at the stake during the reign of Queen Mary Tudor.

A. Thomas Wyatt
B. Martin Luther
C. Edmund Campion
D. Thomas Cranmer

6. Queen Mary was succeeded by her half sister:

A. Elizabeth.
B. Mary, Queen of Scots.
C. Catherine of Aragon.
D. Princess Martha.

7. In 1570, Queen Elizabeth was excommunicated by:

A. Pope Leo X.
B. Pope St. Pius X.
C. Pope St. Pius V.
D. Blessed Pius IX.

8. The Penal Laws made it a crime to:

A. deny Transubstantiation.
B. convert to Protestantism.
C. deny that the pope was the head of the Church on earth.
D. convert to Catholicism.

9. In the story, Father Cottam was traveling disguised as a:

A. jeweler.
B. royal spy.
C. cloth merchant.
D. spice dealer.

10. One of Elizabeth's enemies was the Spanish king:

A. Philip II.
B. Ferdinand.
C. Fernando III.
D. Sancho II.

True or False?

Directions: In the blank beside each statement, write "T" if the statement is *True* or "F" if the statement is *False*. Each correct answer is worth 5 points. 50 possible points.

_____ 1. Edward VI tried to make England Catholic again.

_____ 2. Mary Tudor was treated very poorly by her father when she was young.

_____ 3. Mary Tudor let Protestant nobles keep the Church lands they had stolen.

_____ 4. Queen Mary was gentler and more forgiving after Wyatt's rebellion.

_____ 5. Sir Thomas Wyatt was beheaded and his body chopped into pieces.

_____ 6. Catholics called Queen Mary "Bloody Mary."

_____ 7. Queen Mary died without an heir.

_____ 8. Queen Elizabeth returned England to Protestantism.

_____ 9. The Penal Laws punished Catholics for remaining loyal to the Church.

____ 10. The Penal Laws stated that priests caught in the Kingdom of England were to be given a warning and set free.

CHAPTER 11
King Philip II

Perfect Score: 100   Your Score: _____

Multiple Choice

Directions: For each numbered item, circle the letter beside the choice (A, B, C, or D) that best answers the question or completes the statement. Circle only one choice per item. Each correct answer is worth 5 points. 25 possible points.

1. During the 1500s, the wealthiest kingdom in Europe was:

A. England.
B. France.
C. Germany.
D. Spain.

2. The phrase *Siglo de Oro* means:

A. Century of Gold.
B. Work and pray.
C. Spanish Armada.
D. Age of Broken Dreams.

3. Philip II was the son of the Holy Roman emperor:

A. Philip I.
B. Charles V.
C. the duke of Alba.
D. Maximilian I.

4. King Philip and Queen Elizabeth were fighting because of a region called the:

A. Escorial.
B. Low Counties.
C. New World.
D. Old Countries.

5. The word *Armada* comes from the Spanish word for:

A. armed.
B. armistice.
C. armpit.
D. navy.

Matching

Directions: In each blank beside a phrase, write the letter of the term that is described by that phrase. Each item is worth 5 points. 75 possible points.

A. Escorial
B. Queen Mary Tudor
C. New World
D. Hieronymite Order
E. cloth

F. Elizabeth
G. The Low Countries
H. The Iron Duke
I. Council of Troubles
J. pirates

K. Spanish Armada
L. Mary, Queen of Scots
M. Ireland
N. English Channel
O. Duke of Alba

_____ 1. Netherlands, Belgium, Flanders, Luxembourg.

_____ 2. A nickname for the duke of Alba.

_____ 3. The palace of Philip II.

_____ 4. He was sent to the Netherlands by King Philip to end the revolt there.

_____ 5. A special court set up to punish those who resisted Spanish rule in the Netherlands.

_____ 6. King Philip was briefly married to her.

_____ 7. Elizabeth sent them to attack Spanish ships.

_____ 8. These monks staffed the Escorial.

_____ 9. Where the Spanish Armada was defeated.

_____ 10. Decided she wanted to be enemies with Spain.

_____ 11. King Philip wanted to put her on the throne of England.

_____ 12. Spanish ships brought gold, sugar, and many other things from here.

_____ 13. In 1588, this was sent to invade England.

_____ 14. Many of the Spanish ships ended up crashing on the coast here.

_____ 15. The merchants of the Low Countries shipped this all over Europe.

CHAPTER 12
The Thirty Years' War

Perfect Score: 100   Your Score: _____

Multiple Choice

Directions: For each numbered item, circle the letter beside the choice (A, B, C, or D) that best answers the question or completes the statement. Circle only one choice per item. Each correct answer is worth 10 points. 100 possible points.

1. King Ferdinand ordered all Protestant churches on royal lands to be closed and handed over to Catholics in what kingdom?

A. France
B. Sweden
C. Denmark
D. Bohemia

2. *Defenestration* means:

A. when someone changes their religion.
B. when soldiers all fire their guns at once.
C. being thrown out a window.
D. to put up a fence.

3. Emperor Ferdinand was suspicious of this general. He fired him and later had him killed.

A. Count Tilly
B. Gustavus Adolphus
C. Baron of Highfall
D. Count Wallenstein

4. This king had spent a lot of time making his army the best in Europe.

A. King Christian IV of Denmark
B. King Gustavus Adolphus of Sweden
C. King Ferdinand of Bohemia
D. Emperor Matthias

5. Firing in a volley means that:

A. every soldier fires his gun whenever he wants.
B. soldiers all shoot their guns up in the air and hope the bullets hit their enemies when they fall.
C. all the soldiers fire their guns in a circular direction.
D. all the soldiers fire their guns at once and in the same direction.

6. At the Battle of Lützen:

A. Wallenstein was defeated and killed.
B. Wallenstein won and Gustavus Adolphus was killed.
C. Emperor Ferdinand lost control of Prague.
D. The usurper Frederick was defeated and Bohemia was conquered.

7. The Peace of Westphalia:

A. ended the Thirty Years' War and gave the Holy Roman emperor much more power.
B. declared that all princes in the Holy Roman Empire must become Catholic.
C. ended the Thirty Years' War and reduced the power of the Holy Roman emperor.
D. declared that all the princes of the Holy Roman Empire must become Lutheran.

8. The king of Denmark who invaded the Holy Roman Empire was:

A. Gustavus Adolphus.
B. King Christian IV.
C. King Frederick.
D. King Ferdinand.

9. The Catholic nobles were thrown out the window in the city of:

A. Prague.
B. Budapest.
C. Munich.
D. Lützen.

10. Catholics said the Catholic nobles survived being thrown out the window because:

A. they landed in a pile of dung.
B. the Blessed Virgin and their guardian angels protected them.
C. they got tangled in some trees on the way down.
D. the fall was only four feet.

CHAPTER 13
Roundheads and Cavaliers

Perfect Score: 100

Your Score: _____

True or False?

Directions: In the blank beside each statement, write "T" if the statement is *True* or "F" if the statement is *False*. Each correct answer is worth 5 points. 50 possible points.

_____ 1. The English Civil War was a war of Protestants against other Protestants.

_____ 2. In the years following the Reformation, Protestant groups continued to split off from one another.

_____ 3. Queen Elizabeth's son was King James I of England.

_____ 4. King James was worse to Catholics than Elizabeth had been.

_____ 5. Guy Fawkes tried to blow up Parliament.

_____ 6. After the Gunpowder Plot, King James got rid of all Elizabeth's anti-Catholic laws.

_____ 7. Guy Fawkes was a Catholic.

_____ 8. King James and Parliament got along very well together.

_____ 9. The English Parliament was made up of the House of Lords and the House of Commons.

_____ 10. The House of Commons was made up of the nobility of the realm.

Multiple Choice

Directions: For each numbered item, circle the letter beside the choice (A, B, C, or D) that best answers the question or completes the statement. Circle only one choice per item. Each correct answer is worth 5 points. 50 possible points.

1. Parliament had control over how much the king was allowed to do what?

A. tax his subjects
B. control the Church
C. enter into treaties
D. eat for dinner

2. The divine right of kings was the belief that:

A. people had the right to kill a king whom they disliked.
B. God wanted kings and parliaments to work together.
C. a king ruled by God's authority alone and did not have to answer to anyone.
D. kings should be worshipped as gods.

3. The Anglican archbishop who introduced more Catholic practices into the Anglican Church was:

A. Charles Stuart.
B. William Laud.
C. Oliver Cromwell.
D. Thomas Pride.

4. Puritans followed the theological teachings of:

A. Martin Luther.
B. John Calvin.
C. Thomas Pride.
D. Martin McFly.

5. King Charles unsuccessfully attempted to:

A. make the Anglican Church more Protestant.
B. have William Laud executed.
C. invade France.
D. arrest his enemies in Parliament.

6. In the civil war, the Parliamentarian side was known as the:

A. Roundheads.
B. Cavaliers.
C. Anglicans.
D. Gustavians.

7. The leader of the Parliamentarian army was:

A. Gustavus Adolphus.
B. Thomas Pride.
C. William Laud.
D. Oliver Cromwell.

8. Cromwell's supporters in Parliament voted to:

A. abolish the House of Lords.
B. get rid of the monarchy.
C. proclaim England a republic.
D. all of the above.

9. Colonel Thomas Pride:

A. arrested all the members of Parliament who supported Cromwell.
B. was put in charge of the royalist army.
C. arrested all the members of Parliament who opposed Cromwell.
D. installed William Laud as archbishop of Canterbury.

10. Cromwell wanted his army to be more like the army of:

A. Colonel Thomas Pride.
B. Gustavus Adolphus.
C. King Charles.
D. Count Wallenstein.

CHAPTER 14
The Restoration and the Not-So-Glorious Revolution

Perfect Score: 100   Your Score: _____

Matching

Directions: In each blank beside a phrase, write the letter of the term that is described by that phrase. Each item is worth 10 points. 100 possible points.

A. King Charles I   E. Lord Protector   I. King James II
B. Oliver Cromwell   F. Puritans   J. William of Orange
C. King Charles II   G. Catholics
D. James Edward Francis   H. Thomas Farriner

_____ 1. In the so-called Glorious Revolution, he replaced James II as king of England.

_____ 2. After the death of Cromwell, he was invited back from exile to take the English throne.

_____ 3. Under Charles II, things got better for this group.

_____ 4. The title Oliver Cromwell took for himself.

_____ 5. The Great Fire of London in 1666 started in his bakery.

_____ 6. The last Catholic king of England. He was overthrown by Protestants in 1688.

_____ 7. Under Charles II, this group was persecuted more and many fled England.

_____ 8. He dissolved Parliament and ruled as dictator of England for five years.

_____ 9. The son of James II, this prince would never be king.

_____ 10. This king of England was imprisoned and beheaded.

CHAPTER 15
The Age of the Sun King

Perfect Score: 100   Your Score: _____

Multiple Choice

Directions: For each numbered item, circle the letter beside the choice (A, B, C, or D) that best answers the question or completes the statement. Circle only one choice per item. Each correct answer is worth 5 points. 80 possible points.

1. King Louis XIV reigned as king of France for:

A. 110 years.
B. 30 years.
C. 18 years.
D. 72 years.

2. When King Louis was little, a mob once:

A. beheaded his father.
B. stormed into his bedroom.
C. demanded he be made king.
D. protested his appointment of so many Catholics to important positions.

3. This churchman helped Louis become a strong ruler.

A. Cardinal Richelieu
B. Pope Clement VII
C. Cardinal Beaton
D. Cardinal Mazarin

4. King Louis XIV distrusted this group and thought they needed to be controlled.

A. nobles
B. peasants
C. clergy
D. English

5. King Louis XIV built himself a magnificent palace at:

A. Escorial.
B. Paris.
C. Versailles.
D. Paray-le-Monial.

6. King Louis XIV was known as the:

A. Emperor of the French.
B. Sun King.
C. Lord of the Dance.
D. King of Hearts.

7. King Louis believed that if the nobles were spending all their time and money at his court, they would not have the ability to:

A. travel to the missions in the New World.
B. stir up heresy.
C. make an alliance with Spain.
D. go home and raise a rebellion.

8. King Louis XIV loved:

A. snails for dinner.
B. manners and etiquette.
C. his Huguenot subjects.
D. giving the nobles money.

9. King Louis spent many years trying to claim the throne of:

A. Spain.
B. England.
C. the Holy Roman Empire.
D. Denmark.

10. In 1685, King Louis XIV revoked this decree.

A. The Peace of Westphalia
B. The Confession of Augsburg
C. The Edict of Milan
D. The Edict of Nantes

11. During the reign of King Louis XIV, more than two hundred thousand of this group left France.

A. Jesuits
B. nobles
C. French Protestants
D. farmers

12. The French monarchy eagerly supported:

A. the Huguenots.
B. the Jesuit missions in the New World.
C. the Franciscan missions of Mexico.
D. the antipope Eugenius V.

13. St. Isaac Jogues and St. Jean de Brébeuf:

A. were martyred by Protestants in the Netherlands.
B. were martyred by Iroquois Indians.
C. rebuked Louis XIV for his immoral lifestyle.
D. received the apparitions of the Sacred Heart.

14. This French saint and theologian promoted consecration to Jesus through the Blessed Virgin Mary.

A. St. Louis de Montfort
B. St. Jean de Brébeuf
C. St. Margaret Mary Alacoque
D. St. Isaac Jogues

15. This saint received apparitions of Christ and promoted devotion to the Sacred Heart.

A. St. Louis de Montfort
B. St. Jean de Brébeuf
C. St. Margaret Mary Alacoque
D. St. Isaac Jogues

16. In the apparitions of the Sacred Heart, Jesus asked for Holy Communions on:

A. first Saturdays.
B. first Fridays.
C. Sundays and Holy Days.
D. first Tuesdays.

True or False?

Directions: In the blank beside each statement, write "T" if the statement is *True* or "F" if the statement is *False*. Each correct answer is worth 5 points. 20 possible points.

_____ 1. The French Church had absolutely zero problems under Louis XIV.

_____ 2. King Louis XIV saw his own personal good as the same as the good of the nation.

_____ 3. King Louis reigned so long that his successor was his great-grandson.

_____ 4. King Louis gave the Huguenots their fortified cities back.

CHAPTER 16
The Turkish Threat

Perfect Score: 100   Your Score: _____

Matching

Directions: In each blank beside a phrase, write the letter of the term that is described by that phrase. Each item is worth 5 points. 100 possible points.

A. Blood Tax
B. Vienna
C. Hapsburgs
D. Leopold
E. Holy Roman Empire
F. Jan Sobieski III
G. Poland

H. Winged Hussars
I. Mehmet IV
J. Julius Caesar
K. Mohács
L. Eugene of Savoy
M. Ottoman Turks
N. Joseph

O. Hungary
P. Belgrade
Q. Serbia
R. Treaty of Passarowitz
S. Istanbul
T. Islam

_____ 1. Polish king who saved Vienna from the Turks.

_____ 2. The religion of the Ottoman Turks.

_____ 3. This dashing prince liberated Hungary and Serbia from the Turks.

_____ 4. Son and successor of Holy Roman Emperor Leopold.

_____ 5. This city was home of the Hapsburgs and was besieged by the Turks in 1683.

_____ 6. The capital of the Ottoman Empire.

_____ 7. This Holy Roman emperor declared war on the Turks and took back much land from them.

_____ 8. This family ruled the Holy Roman Empire.

_____ 9. After his victory at Vienna, King Jan Sobieski III quoted this famous person, though he changed the quote to give God credit.

_____ 10. In 1717, Christians took this capital city of Serbia from the Turks.

_____ 11. This gave Serbia to the Holy Roman Empire.

_____ 12. The famous Polish cavalry.

_____ 13. Turkish sultan who attacked the Holy Roman Empire.

_____ 14. Belgrade was the capital of this kingdom.

_____ 15. A practice where Christian boys were taken from their homes by the Turks, converted to Islam, and forced to become soldiers.

_____ 16. Jan Sobieski III was king of this country.

_____ 17. At this battle, imperial generals counterattacked a Turkish charge, turning it into a Christian victory.

_____ 18. This kingdom declared war on the Ottoman Empire and took many Christian lands back.

_____ 19. After the Battle of Mohács, the Turks lost control of this kingdom.

_____ 20. They were the traditional enemies of Christian Europe.

CHAPTER 17
The Jacobites

Perfect Score: 100

Your Score: _____

True or False?

Directions: In the blank beside each statement, write "T" if the statement is *True* or "F" if the statement is *False*. Each correct answer is worth 10 points. 100 possible points.

_____ 1. By 1700, the destructive religious wars of the Reformation era had ceased.

_____ 2. Those who wanted King James and the Stuarts returned to the throne of England were called Jacobites.

_____ 3. Though the English and Scots shared a single crown, the two kingdoms always remained separate.

_____ 4. The Scottish Jacobites supported the Hanoverians.

_____ 5. To emigrate means to leave one's country to permanently settle in another.

_____ 6. Bonnie Prince Charlie was the Old Pretender.

_____ 7. Bonnie Prince Charlie was defeated by Duke William of Cumberland at Culloden Moor.

_____ 8. A royal pretender is someone who claims to be king or queen but is not recognized as a true ruler.

_____ 9. Flora MacDonald helped Bonnie Prince Charlie escape back to France.

_____ 10. The British respected Scottish culture and encouraged traditional Scottish customs.

CHAPTER 18
Light and Darkness

Perfect Score: 100   Your Score: _____

Multiple Choice

Directions: For each numbered item, circle the letter beside the choice (A, B, C, or D) that best answers the question or completes the statement. Circle only one choice per item. Each correct answer is worth 5 points. 100 possible points.

1. Some of the greatest changes in the 1600s and 1700s were how people thought about:

A. farming.
B. travel.
C. science.
D. cooking.

2. This invention made it easier for scientists and inventors to write about their discoveries.

A. mechanical clock
B. printing press
C. books
D. water wheel

3. Scientific academies were places where:

A. scientific experiments were carried out.
B. college students were taught science classes.
C. scientists were buried after they died.
D. scientists would meet to read each other's writings and discuss new ideas.

4. The age of scientific discovery in the 1600s and 1700s is often called the:

A. Enlightenment.
B. Renaissance.
C. Modern World.
D. Endarkenment.

5. The circulation of blood through the body was discovered by:

A. William Harvey.
B. Isaac Newton.
C. Antonie van Leeuwenhoek.
D. Galileo.

6. The first microscope was invented by:

A. Isaac Newton.
B. Galileo.
C. Antonie van Leeuwenhoek.
D. Nicolaus Copernicus.

7. Isaac Newton's book the *Principia* contained:

A. detailed drawings of microscopic bacteria.
B. a theory of the earth's rotation around the sun.
C. an explanation of the basic laws of motion.
D. a diagram of the human circulatory system.

8. Nicolaus Copernicus's theory of heliocentrism taught that:

A. the earth revolves around the sun.
B. the sun revolves around the earth.
C. a force called gravity holds all things together.
D. objects of different weights will fall at the same speed.

9. Galileo's law of free fall taught that:

A. heavier objects fall faster.
B. objects fall at the same speed because the earth itself pulls them.
C. gravity pulls all things apart.
D. everything is made up of tiny particles called atoms.

10. Galileo is best known for his invention of the:

A. stethoscope.
B. microscope.
C. hydroscope.
D. telescope.

11. Galileo angered Church authorities by:

A. talking about science.
B. being a scientist.
C. inventing the telescope.
D. writing a book that portrayed churchmen as simpletons and idiots.

12. This German Jesuit made important discoveries in geology, biology, and medicine.

A. Galileo Galilei.
B. Athanasius Kircher.
C. Antonie van Leeuwenhoek.
D. Nicolaus Stenson.

13. René-Just Haüy was one of the first scientists to study:

A. blood circulation.
B. geology.
C. the salivary gland.
D. crystals.

14. Nicolaus Stenson:

A. wrote *The Revolutions of the Heavenly Spheres*.
B. was known as the "Master of a Hundred Arts."
C. studied the bodies of animals and discovered the salivary gland.
D. wrote the *Principia*.

15. Some Enlightenment thinkers were hostile to:

A. new ideas.
B. religion.
C. the monarchy.
D. scientific knowledge.

16. The belief that God exists but never gets involved in human affairs is called:

A. deism.
B. atheism.
C. heliocentrism.
D. geocentrism.

17. Indifferentism is the belief that:

A. the sun revolves around the earth.
B. God does not perform miracles.
C. one religion is just as good as another.
D. as sands slip through the hourglass, so are the days of our lives.

18. Despite the scientific advances of the Enlightenment, this suffered.

A. education
B. faith
C. monarchy
D. the academies

19. An encyclopedia of scientific knowledge ridiculing religion was written by:

A. Voltaire.
B. Athanasius Kircher.
C. Denis Diderot.
D. René-Just Haüy.

20. Galileo believed the theories of this man were correct.

A. Diderot
B. Stenson
C. Aristotle
D. Copernicus

CHAPTER 19
A World at War

Perfect Score: 100   Your Score: _____

Matching

Directions: In each blank beside a phrase, write the letter of the term that is described by that phrase. Each item is worth 5 points. 50 possible points.

A. French and   C. Ballistics   F. France   I. Quiberon Bay
     Indian War   D. Ohio Valley   G. George III   J. Wealth, prestige,
B. Edward Hawke   E. plunder   H. colony   and power

_____ 1. The study of firearms.

_____ 2. A piece of land under the control of another country.

_____ 3. Why Europeans wanted colonies.

_____ 4. The Seven Years' War in North America began over this piece of land.

_____ 5. In the United States, the Seven Years' War was known by this name.

_____ 6. The violent acquisition of property or other stolen goods.

_____ 7. This was one of the most important naval battles of the Seven Years' War.

_____ 8. This country lost the Seven Years' War and had to give up its North American possessions.

_____ 9. King of Great Britain during the American Revolution.

_____ 10. The British victor of Quiberon Bay.

True or False?

Directions: In the blank beside each statement, write "T" if the statement is *True* or "F" if the statement is *False*. Each correct answer is worth 5 points. 50 possible points.

_____ 1. After the Seven Years' War, Britain had lots of money.

_____ 2. The war against the American colonies was unpopular in Britain.

_____ 3. The British Parliament wanted to tax the North American colonies to help pay for the cost of the war.

_____ 4. George Washington had to surrender his army to the British general Cornwallis.

_____ 5. The Treaty of Paris recognized the independence of the American colonies.

_____ 6. The Seven Years' War was fought in many different countries.

_____ 7. The Seven Years' War was motivated by Christian ideals.

_____ 8. During the 1700s, European armies became much stronger.

_____ 9. During the 1700s, huge chunks of the world began to come under European power.

_____ 10. The Seven Years' War was the first true "world war" in history.

CHAPTER 20
The French Revolution

Perfect Score: 100   Your Score: _____

Multiple Choice

Directions: For each numbered item, circle the letter beside the choice (A, B, C, or D) that best answers the question or completes the statement. Circle only one choice per item. Each correct answer is worth 10 points. 100 possible points.

1. These radical revolutionaries wanted to get rid of both the monarchy and Christianity.

A. First Estate
B. National Assembly
C. Jacobites
D. Jacobins

2. This French king was overthrown and beheaded.

A. George III
B. Louis XIV
C. Louis XVI
D. Robespierre

3. The Third Estate renamed themselves the:

A. Second Estate.
B. Directory.
C. Committee of Public Safety.
D. National Assembly.

4. This was a kind of grand council of all the important people in France.

A. Parliament
B. First Estate
C. Continental Congress
D. Estates General

5. The National Assembly:

A. restricted the king's power.
B. took control of the army.
C. abolished many old laws and customs.
D. all of the above.

6. To nationalize something means:

A. to give it to the people.
B. to put little flags all over it.
C. to put the government in control of it.
D. to shut it down.

7. Under the National Assembly, monasteries and convents:

A. were closed.
B. saw record numbers of vocations.
C. were forced to pay heavy fines.
D. were painted red, white, and blue.

8. Maximilien Robespierre was in charge of the:

A. National Assembly.
B. Committee of Public Safety.
C. Archdiocese of Paris.
D. Vendée.

9. The purpose of the guillotine was to:

A. assess taxes on the French people.
B. chop people's heads off.
C. reform the laws of France.
D. put down riots.

10. The general appointed by the Directory to put down a royalist revolt was:

A. Maximilien Robespierre.
B. Étienne Gilson.
C. Jacques Tempier.
D. Napoleon Bonaparte.

CHAPTER 21
The Rise and Fall of Napoleon

Perfect Score: 100   Your Score: _____

Matching

Directions: In each blank beside a phrase, write the letter of the term that is described by that phrase. Each item is worth 5 points. 100 possible points.

A. Egypt
B. Turks
C. Horatio Nelson
D. coup
E. Directory
F. First Consul

G. squares
H. concordat
I. Pope Pius VII
J. Emperor of the French
K. Notre Dame

L. Papal States
M. Russia
N. Grand Armée
O. Nicholas II
P. Moscow
Q. Louis XVIII

R. Duke of Wellington
S. Waterloo
T. St. Helena

_____ 1. Napoleon was finally defeated at this battle by the British and the Prussians.

_____ 2. Napoleon had himself crowned this by the pope.

_____ 3. In 1799, Napoleon returned to France and overthrew this group.

_____ 4. When someone overthrows the government and replaces it with a new one.

_____ 5. The tsar of Russia.

_____ 6. An agreement between the Church and a government.

_____ 7. French soldiers fought in this formation.

_____ 8. After the fall of Napoleon, he was proclaimed king of France.

_____ 9. Napoleon spent his last days in exile on this island.

_____ 10. The army of Napoleon, with which he invaded Russia.

_____ 11. The Directory sent Napoleon to conquer this land from the Turks.

_____ 12. This British admiral destroyed the French fleet.

_____ 13. After Napoleon took power, he gave himself this title, calling to mind the ancient Roman republic.

_____ 14. This pope was kidnapped by Napoleon.

_____ 15. This British commander was the victor of the Battle of Waterloo.

_____ 16. Napoleon's imperial coronation took place in this cathedral.

_____ 17. When Napoleon captured this city, he was puzzled to find it abandoned.

_____ 18. Napoleon's greatest mistake was invading this country.

_____ 19. When Napoleon came to Egypt, it was being ruled by this group.

_____ 20. Napoleon took these away from the pope.

CHAPTER 22
Peace Returns

Perfect Score: 100   Your Score: _____

Multiple Choice

Directions: For each numbered item, circle the letter beside the choice (A, B, C, or D) that best answers the question or completes the statement. Circle only one choice per item. Each correct answer is worth 10 points. 100 possible points.

1. After Napoleon's wars, the great powers of Europe had this meeting to decide how to reorganize the continent.

A. French Revolution
B. Congress of Vienna
C. Concordat
D. Continental Congress

2. The idea of "balance of power" was that:

A. the British Empire should be the most powerful.
B. France should be reduced and divided so it could never cause trouble again.
C. one nation should never be allowed to get too powerful.
D. Russia should produce all the vodka in Europe.

3. The most talented diplomat at the Congress of Vienna was:

A. St. John Vianney.
B. the duke of Wellington.
C. Napoleon.
D. Prince Metternich.

4. The four most important kingdoms at the Congress of Vienna were:

A. Britain, Austria, Prussia, and Russia.
B. Britain, France, Russia, and Italy.
C. the Ottoman Empire, Prussia, Denmark, and Britain.
D. England, Wales, Scotland, and Ireland.

5. The Holy Alliance was a political alliance of:

A. Britain, Prussia, and France.
B. Prussia, Italy, and Britain.
C. Russia, Austria, and Britain.
D. Prussia, Russia, and Austria.

6. Metternich's idea of conservatism meant that:

A. the traditional way of things should not be changed too much.
B. there should be violent, radical change.
C. the Church must be weakened.
D. no one country should become too powerful.

7. Prince Metternich was from:

A. Britain.
B. Russia.
C. Prussia.
D. Austria.

8. *Curé* is a French word for:

A. medicine.
B. congress.
C. pastor.
D. bishop.

9. This famous French saint from Ars was known as a miracle worker and confessor.

A. St. John Nepomucene
B. St. John Vianney
C. St. Margaret Mary
D. St. Padre Pio

10. In many places, the presence of occupying French troops had made people:

A. abandon Catholicism.
B. realize how crummy their own countries were.
C. want weaker armies.
D. have patriotic feelings about their own countries.

CHAPTER 23
Reforms and Revolutions

Perfect Score: 100   Your Score: _____

True or False?

Directions: In the blank beside each statement, write "T" if the statement is *True* or "F" if the statement is *False*. Each correct answer is worth 10 points. 100 possible points.

_____ 1. Though much of the fighting was over by this period in European history, forces had been unleashed that could not be contained.

_____ 2. The ideas of the Enlightenment were causing people to slowly lose faith in the Christian message.

_____ 3. Liberals were people who wanted their kings and queens to have more power and for the people to have less.

_____ 4. A democratic government means voters elect people to make their laws.

_____ 5. The British Corn Laws kept the price of grain low and were popular with the people.

_____ 6. In 1819, British soldiers killed liberal protestors in Manchester, England.

_____ 7. King Charles X of France was a liberal king who embraced the ideas of the revolution.

_____ 8. Louis-Philippe was known as the Citizen King.

_____ 9. The constitution of Louis-Philippe proclaimed Catholicism the official religion of France.

_____ 10. President Louis-Napoleon Bonaparte became Emperor Napoleon III.

CHAPTER 24
The Unification of Italy and Germany

Perfect Score: 100

Your Score: _____

Multiple Choice

Directions: For each numbered item, circle the letter beside the choice (A, B, C, or D) that best answers the question or completes the statement. Circle only one choice per item. Each correct answer is worth 5 points. 25 possible points.

1. Otto von Bismarck:

A. unified Italy.
B. published the *Communist Manifesto*.
C. was a German shipbuilder.
D. helped build and solidify the Prussian Empire.

2. The Franco-Prussian War:

A. was a resounding victory for France.
B. saw Russians and Prussians on the same side of the war.
C. was won by the Prussians using telegraph lines and railroads.
D. resulted in the execution of the French king.

3. The *Communist Manifesto*:

A. was written by Karl Marx and Friedrich Engels.
B. was written by Joseph Stalin and Vladimir Lenin.
C. was accepted by Pope Pius IX.
D. said that dictatorship was the best form of government.

4. The Kingdom of Italy:

A. took into account the needs of the Church.
B. was complete once the Papal States were under the control of the king.
C. was ruled by Garibaldi.
D. wasn't established until 1900.

5. Pope Pius IX:

A. greatly supported the unification of Italy.
B. was a personal friend of Garibaldi.
C. wrote a strongly worded letter condemning the new government.
D. died during the attack on Rome by the Kingdom of Italy.

True or False?

Directions: In the blank beside each statement, write "T" if the statement is *True* or "F" if the statement is *False*. Each correct answer is worth 5 points. 25 possible points.

_____ 1. Two Russians wrote the *Communist Manifesto.*

_____ 2. Bismarck and Garibaldi became the kings of Germany and Italy, respectively.

_____ 3. Wilhelm and Victor Emmanuel became the kings of Germany and Italy, respectively.

_____ 4. Pope Pius IX refused to give up the Papal States and was attacked by Italy.

_____ 5. Communists wanted to steal from the rich and give to the poor but went about it by killing.

Matching

Directions: In each blank beside a phrase, write the letter of the term that is described by that phrase. Each item is worth 5 points. 50 possible points.

A. Communism
B. Kaiser Wilhelm I
C. Karl Marx
D. atheism

E. Giuseppe Garibaldi
F. Franco-Prussian War
G. Napoleon III
H. Otto von Bismarck

I. Victor Emmanuel
J. Pope Pius IX

_____ 1. One author of the *Communist Manifesto*.

_____ 2. Chancellor of the united German Empire.

_____ 3. King of the united Italian kingdom.

_____ 4. Wrote an angry letter condemning the Italian kingdom.

_____ 5. Anti-Christian ideal system that taught that the rich always oppress the poor.

_____ 6. Belief that there is no God.

_____ 7. Italian nationalist who helped unite the Kingdom of Italy.

_____ 8. Emperor of Germany.

_____ 9. This armed conflict helped unify Germany and Italy.

_____ 10. Nephew of the great French leader Napoleon.

CHAPTER 25
The Popes Against the World

Perfect Score: 100   Your Score: _____

True or False?

Directions: In the blank beside each statement, write "T" if the statement is *True* or "F" if the statement is *False*. Each correct answer is worth 5 points. 50 possible points.

_____ 1. Pope Pius IX supported a united Italy.

_____ 2. The doctrine of Papal Infallibility was taught at the First Vatican Council.

_____ 3. Pope Leo XIII wrote the St. Michael prayer after a vision.

_____ 4. The teaching of the Catholic Church changes with the times.

_____ 5. Persecution of the Church by the British government continued well into the 1900s.

_____ 6. Modernism is a heresy condemned by the Church.

_____ 7. Liberalism and Communism were two ideas opposed to the Church during this period.

_____ 8. The "Prisoner of the Vatican" refers to the popes in the late 1800s through the early 1900s who never left the Vatican grounds.

_____ 9. The First Vatican Council was the first time the Church ever believed in Papal Infallibility.

_____ 10. Strong popes and bishops helped the Church survive the challenges of revolution and modernism.

Matching

Directions: In each blank beside a phrase, write the letter of the term that is described by that phrase. Each item is worth 5 points. 50 possible points.

A. Pope Pius X
B. Pope Pius IX
C. Pope Leo XIII

D. St. Michael prayer
E. prisoners of the Vatican

F. Otto von Bismarck
G. Third French Republic

H. Modernism
I. Great Britain
J. working poor

_____ 1. Pope who had a terrifying vision in 1884.

_____ 2. Taught that the Church's teachings should evolve with the times.

_____ 3. Called the First Vatican Council.

_____ 4. Pope Leo XIII was very concerned about their sufferings.

_____ 5. Given in a vision to a pope.

_____ 6. Attempted to weaken the Church in Germany.

_____ 7. Nickname given to popes who refused to leave Vatican City.

_____ 8. Pope who named Modernism a heresy.

_____ 9. Allowed for Catholic bishops to return in 1850.

_____ 10. Passed anti-Catholic laws in France.

CHAPTER 26
Europe Conquers the Globe

Perfect Score: 100

Your Score: _____

Multiple Choice

Directions: For each numbered item, circle the letter beside the choice (A, B, C, or D) that best answers the question or completes the statement. Circle only one choice per item. Each correct answer is worth 10 points. 50 possible points.

1. European colonialism:

A. resulted in nothing but good things for the world.
B. subjugated all Christians to Rome.
C. had both positive and negative effects on the world.
D. was a duty, according to God.

2. Great Britain:

A. ruled the entire world in the late 1800s.
B. was kicked out of China and India due to violent rebellions.
C. killed many Chinese Catholics in the Boxer Rebellion.
D. had the largest colonial empire of all European countries.

3. The Sepoy Munity:

A. took place in the early 1900s.
B. was fought between the Fists of Righteousness and the British.
C. cost the lives of eight hundred thousand Indians and six thousand Europeans.
D. was condemned by the United States.

4. The Boxer Rebellion:

A. was a Chinese revolt against foreigners.
B. was an Indian revolt against the British.
C. targeted Muslims in their attacks.
D. was a peaceful protest that ended in the British relinquishing control of China.

5. The European countries that subjugated the rest of the world:

A. were always kind to their conquered subjects.
B. never seized the natural resources of the land they occupied.
C. were often welcomed by the native peoples.
D. were fulfilling a special obligation, according to Rudyard Kipling.

Matching

Directions: In each blank beside a phrase, write the letter of the term that is described by that phrase. Each item is worth 10 points. 50 possible points.

A. Ironclads and automatic   B. Fists of Righteousness   D. Sepoy Mutiny
     weapons   C. 1800s and 1900s   E. Great Britain

_____ 1. Rebels in China who wanted foreigners out.

_____ 2. Largest colonial empire in the world.

_____ 3. Era of more aggressive colonialization.

_____ 4. Weapons that allowed for European domination.

_____ 5. Rebellion in India against the British.

CHAPTER 27
The Great War

Perfect Score: 100   Your Score: _____

True or False?

Directions: In the blank beside each statement, write "T" if the statement is *True* or "F" if the statement is *False*. Each correct answer is worth 5 points. 50 possible points.

_____ 1. The Allies of the Great War were Britain, France, and Germany.

_____ 2. Kaiser Wilhelm II was the head of the German Empire at the start of the Great War.

_____ 3. The Ottoman Empire was one of the Central Powers.

_____ 4. Archduke Franz Ferdinand was killed by a French spy.

_____ 5. Great Britain attacked Germany because Germany attacked Belgium.

_____ 6. Italy fought on the side of the Central Powers.

_____ 7. Technology changed how armies fought in the Great War.

_____ 8. The Lady of Fatima appeared before the Great War began and predicted it.

_____ 9. The United States entered the war on the side of the Allies.

_____ 10. Germany remained an empire after the war.

Matching

Directions: In each blank beside a phrase, write the letter of the term that is described by that phrase. Each item is worth 5 points. 50 possible points.

A. Allies
B. Kaiser Wilhelm II
C. Our Lady of Fatima
D. machine guns

E. Pope Pius X
F. Archduke Franz
    Ferdinand
G. Sarajevo

H. Central Powers
I. Russia
J. the Great War

_____ 1. City where Archduke Franz Ferdinand was killed.

_____ 2. Britain, France, Italy, and later the United States.

_____ 3. New weapons that changed how war was fought.

_____ 4. Joined the Allies to fight the Central Powers.

_____ 5. Fell ill and died at the start of the Great War.

_____ 6. His assassination led to the outbreak of the Great War.

_____ 7. Leader of the German Empire during the war.

_____ 8. Germany, the Austro-Hungarian Empire, and the Ottoman Empire.

_____ 9. War that enveloped Europe from 1914 to 1918.

____ 10. Apparition of Mary to three shepherds in 1917.

CHAPTER 28
The Rise of the Dictators

Perfect Score: 100   Your Score: _____

Multiple Choice

Directions: For each numbered item, circle the letter beside the choice (A, B, C, or D) that best answers the question or completes the statement. Circle only one choice per item. Each correct answer is worth 5 points. 25 possible points.

1. The Treaty of Versailles:

A. penalized England for starting the Great War.
B. dedicated France to the Blessed Mother.
C. punished Germany severely.
D. ended the French Revolution.

2. After the war, the Ottoman Turks:

A. ruled Austria-Hungary's old territory.
B. began their career as furniture craftsmen.
C. became a Communist dictatorship.
D. lost their empire and became a republic.

3. Vladimir Lenin:

A. led the Bolsheviks in the Russian Revolution.
B. was a general in the Russian army.
C. gave his rivals great advancement in the Communist government.
D. was a benevolent leader of Russia.

4. Italian Fascism:

A. was ideologically similar to democracy.
B. was opposed to both Communism and democracy.
C. was symbolized by the Roman laurel wreath.
D. was led by the pope.

5. Adolf Hitler:

A. rose to power in Italy.
B. was sympathetic to the Jews in Germany.
C. led the Nazi party in Germany and became chancellor.
D. fought for Britain during World War I.

True or False?

Directions: In the blank beside each statement, write "T" if the statement is *True* or "F" if the statement is *False*. Each correct answer is worth 5 points. 25 possible points.

_____ 1. Germany became a republic after the war.

_____ 2. The Russian Revolution turned Russia into a democracy.

_____ 3. The Bolsheviks killed the tsar of Russia and his family during the revolution.

_____ 4. The Fascists and the Communists fought in the streets in Italy.

_____ 5. Adolf Hitler became King Adolf I of Germany in 1933.

Matching

Directions: In each blank beside a phrase, write the letter of the term that is described by that phrase. Each item is worth 5 points. 50 possible points.

A. Nicholas II
B. Treaty of Versailles
C. USSR
D. Vladimir Lenin
E. Bolsheviks
F. *Il Duce*
G. Blackshirts
H. Nazis
I. Weimar Republic
J. Victor Emmanuel III

_____ 1. United Soviet Socialist Republics.

_____ 2. The Fascists in Italy.

_____ 3. The German government after the Great War.

_____ 4. Tsar during the Russian Revolution.

_____ 5. The National Socialist German Workers Party.

_____ 6. Leader of the Russian revolutionaries and head of the USSR.

_____ 7. King of Italy during the rise of Mussolini.

_____ 8. Treaty that punished Germany for World War I.

_____ 9. Group that overthrew the Russian government during World War I.

_____ 10. Means "the Leader."

CHAPTER 29
The Second World War

Perfect Score: 100   Your Score: _____

Matching

Directions: In each blank beside a phrase, write the letter of the term that is described by that phrase. Each item is worth 10 points. 100 possible points.

A. Joseph Stalin   E. Mussolini   I. concentration camps
B. 1939   F. Nazi invasion of Poland   J. Stalingrad
C. Blitzkrieg   G. Third Reich
D. League of Nations   H. Neville Chamberlain

_____ 1. Formed after World War I to prevent future war.

_____ 2. Another name for the Nazi state.

_____ 3. Prime minister of Britain who negotiated with Hitler.

_____ 4. Lighting War.

_____ 5. Camps where the Nazis imprisoned those they deemed "undesirable."

_____ 6. Communist dictator of Russia.

_____ 7. Battle lost by Germany in Russia that forced their retreat.

_____ 8. Joined with Hitler to protect Italy.

_____ 9. Year World War II began.

_____ 10. This led the Allies to declare war on Germany.

CHAPTER 30
The Third Reich Collapses

Perfect Score: 100   Your Score: _____

Multiple Choice

Directions: For each numbered item, circle the letter beside the choice (A, B, C, or D) that best answers the question or completes the statement. Circle only one choice per item. Each correct answer is worth 5 points. 25 possible points.

1. Genocide is:

A. the extermination of a race or culture.
B. a type of poison.
C. a method of warfare used against Germany in World War II.
D. the act of killing a leader.

2. Pope Pius XII:

A. supported the Nazis in their beliefs.
B. betrayed the Faith and the Jews living in Rome.
C. was honored by the Jews after the war for his attempts to save them.
D. was killed by the Nazis.

3. St. Maximilian Kolbe:

A. was a pope.
B. offered his life for another man's in a concentration camp.
C. was a famous soldier in World War II.
D. became a bishop after the war was over.

4. America landed its army in Europe on D-Day, June 6:

A. 1945.
B. 1938.
C. 1944.
D. 1918.

5. Adolf Hitler:

A. surrendered to Russia in 1945.
B. was shot by the Allies as he defended his bunker.
C. stood trial after the war for his crimes.
D. killed himself in 1945.

True or False?

Directions: In the blank beside each statement, write "T" if the statement is *True* or "F" if the statement is *False*. Each correct answer is worth 5 points. 25 possible points.

_____ 1. The Russian army was the first to reach Berlin.

_____ 2. When Hitler died, World War II was over.

_____ 3. America entered the war after Japan bombed Pearl Harbor.

_____ 4. St. Maximilian Kolbe is a martyr.

_____ 5. The SS and Nazi party leaders were put on trial at Nuremberg.

Matching

Directions: In each blank beside a phrase, write the letter of the term that is described by that phrase. Each item is worth 5 points. 50 possible points.

A. SS
B. Holocaust
C. May 7, 1945
D. Pope Pius XII

E. genocide
F. Winston Churchill
G. Auschwitz
H. Pearl Harbor

I. Franklin D. Roosevelt
J. D-Day

_____ 1. A name for the day the Allies landed at Normandy.

_____ 2. Name for the killing of six million Jews under the Third Reich.

_____ 3. Death camp where St. Maximilian Kolbe died.

_____ 4. Site of the attack that brought the United States into the war.

_____ 5. Group under Hitler that sought out and killed Jews.

_____ 6. The killing of so many Jews by the Nazis is an example of _____.

_____ 7. Hid Jews in the Vatican when the Nazis came to Rome.

_____ 8. Leader of Britain during World War II.

_____ 9. Leader of the United States during World War II.

____ 10. Date of the surrender of Germany.

CHAPTER 31
The Cold War

Perfect Score: 100   Your Score: _____

Multiple Choice

Directions: For each numbered item, circle the letter beside the choice (A, B, C, or D) that best answers the question or completes the statement. Circle only one choice per item. Each correct answer is worth 5 points. 25 possible points.

1. Hiroshima and Nagasaki were:

A. twin brothers.
B. the targets of the first two atomic bomb attacks.
C. German coastal cities.
D. ancient Japanese warriors.

2. World War II ended in:

A. 1994.
B. 1947.
C. 1945.
D. 1918.

3. The Berlin Wall:

A. was constructed in 1949.
B. divided the city of Berlin in two.
C. was constructed by the democratic West.
D. kept Russia out of Germany.

4. The Iron Curtain:

A. was a new weapon developed by the United States.
B. hung in Stalin's bedroom.
C. was actually made of steel, concrete, and barbed wire.
D. was the metaphor for the divide between the Communist East and the Free West.

5. The Cold War:

A. was fought in the Arctic tundra by Inuit tribes.
B. resulted in global warming.
C. was "fought" by the superpowers so as to avoid using their nuclear weapons.
D. ended in nuclear war.

True or False?

Directions: In the blank beside each statement, write "T" if the statement is *True* or "F" if the statement is *False*. Each correct answer is worth 5 points. 25 possible points.

_____ 1. The United States dropped food to East Berlin in 1949.

_____ 2. The atomic bombs dropped on Japan killed sixty million people.

_____ 3. Joseph Stalin promised that the Eastern European countries would have free elections.

_____ 4. Great Britain was the first nation to invent the nuclear bomb.

_____ 5. Eighty Germans were killed by the Communists as they tried to cross the Berlin Wall.

Matching

Directions: In each blank beside a phrase, write the letter of the term that is described by that phrase. Each item is worth 5 points. 50 possible points.

A. Cold War
B. Hiroshima
C. Joseph Stalin
D. Stasi

E. atomic bomb
F. superpowers
G. Berlin Wall
H. East Germany

I. Berlin Airlift
J. nuclear weapons

_____ 1. Dictator of Communist Russia.

_____ 2. Two of these were dropped on Japan in 1945.

_____ 3. Controlled by the Communists in the wake of World War II.

_____ 4. A long period of tension between the United States and the Soviet Union.

_____ 5. Weapons capable of destroying human civilization entirely.

_____ 6. Russian secret police.

_____ 7. Countries that have nuclear capabilities.

_____ 8. The target of the first atomic bomb.

_____ 9. Brought food to starving citizens of East Berlin.

_____ 10. Divided East Germany from West Germany.

CHAPTER 32
Changes in the Modern World

Perfect Score: 100   Your Score: _____

Matching

Directions: In each blank beside a phrase, write the letter of the term that is described by that phrase. Each item is worth 10 points. 50 possible points.

A. monarchy   D. hedonism
B. computers   E. technology
C. nationalism

_____ 1. When the government takes control of an industry.

_____ 2. Largely disappeared after World War I.

_____ 3. Advanced rapidly in the 1950s and 1960s.

_____ 4. In the 1960s, these could take up whole rooms.

_____ 5. Living for pleasure.

True or False?

Directions: In the blank beside each statement, write "T" if the statement is *True* or "F" if the statement is *False*. Each correct answer is worth 10 points. 50 possible points.

_____ 1. In Eastern Europe, the Church thrived under Communism.

_____ 2. Technology advanced rapidly in the mid-twentieth century.

_____ 3. Cures for many diseases were found in the 50s and 60s.

_____ 4. Many countries nationalized their industries.

_____ 5. The modern age, with all its technology and conveniences, made worship of God a priority.

CHAPTER 33
The Second Vatican Council

Perfect Score: 100

Your Score: _____

Multiple Choice

Directions: For each numbered item, circle the letter beside the choice (A, B, C, or D) that best answers the question or completes the statement. Circle only one choice per item. Each correct answer is worth 5 points. 25 possible points.

1. As the Church weakened in Europe:

A. it grew stronger elsewhere, in places like Africa and Asia.
B. it grew weaker everywhere else.
C. the popes did nothing.
D. Europe became a better place.

2. Pope John XXIII:

A. thought the Church needed to change its teachings.
B. called the First Vatican Council.
C. wanted to update the way the Church presented its teachings.
D. died after completing Vatican II.

3. The transition from the traditional Latin Mass to the *Novus Ordo*:

A. was welcomed by all in the Church.
B. led to some confusion and controversy.
C. began in 1978.
D. resulted in the collapse of the Catholic Church.

4. The *Novus Ordo*:

A. is irreverent and disrespectful.
B. is said in Latin.
C. resulted in Gregorian chants disappearing from the Mass almost entirely.
D. was written by Pope John Paul II.

5. Toward the end of the twentieth century, poorer nations:

A. became fabulously wealthy.
B. saw the Faith grow in strength.
C. grew more atheistic.
D. refused to adapt to the new Mass.

True or False?

Directions: In the blank beside each statement, write "T" if the statement is *True* or "F" if the statement is *False*. Each correct answer is worth 5 points. 50 possible points.

_____ 1. People continue to debate what the Second Vatican Council actually envisioned.

_____ 2. Vatican II was completed under the leadership of Pope Paul VI.

_____ 3. Pope John XXIII said, "The substance of the ancient doctrine of the deposit of faith is one thing, and the way in which it is presented is another."

_____ 4. Pope Pius XII was succeeded by Pope John XXIII.

_____ 5. Vatican II lasted for ten years.

_____ 6. *Novus Ordo Missae* means "new order of the Mass."

_____ 7. After Vatican II and the *Novus Ordo*, more people went to Mass and joined the religious life.

_____ 8. Vatican II proposed a deeper focus on personal holiness and unity within the Church.

_____ 9. The *Novus Ordo* Mass was drafted as a part of Vatican II.

_____ 10. Vatican II changed the Church's teachings on many subjects.

Matching

Directions: In each blank beside a phrase, write the letter of the term that is described by that phrase. Each item is worth 5 points. 25 possible points.

A. Gregorian chant
B. Pope Paul VI
C. Pope John XXIII

D. *Novus Ordo Missae*
E. vocations

_____ 1. Pope who called the Second Vatican Council.

_____ 2. Pope who brought the Second Vatican Council to a close.

_____ 3. The new order of the Mass, promulgated by Pope Paul VI.

_____ 4. Nearly disappeared from the Mass after Vatican II.

_____ 5. Decreased after the Second Vatican Council.

CHAPTER 34
The End of the Cold War

Perfect Score: 100   Your Score: _____

Matching

Directions: In each blank beside a phrase, write the letter of the term that is described by that phrase. Each item is worth 5 points. 50 possible points.

A. Algeria
B. colonies
C. Third World countries
D. Pope John Paul II
E. Mehmet Ali Ağca

F. the Berlin Wall
G. Communism
H. USSR
I. Karol Wojtyla
J. Poland

_____ 1. Fell in 1989 after twenty-eight years.

_____ 2. Pope who fought Communism.

_____ 3. French colony in North Africa that was granted independence after a bloody war.

_____ 4. Another name for Communist Russia.

_____ 5. Assassin of Pope John Paul II.

_____ 6. Most of these were granted independence in the twentieth century.

_____ 7. Home country of Pope John Paul II.

_____ 8. Usually associated with poverty and corrupt government.

_____ 9. The man who would become Pope John Paul II.

_____ 10. Centered in Russia and defeated with the fall of the USSR.

True or False?

Directions: In the blank beside each statement, write "T" if the statement is *True* or "F" if the statement is *False*. Each correct answer is worth 5 points. 50 possible points.

_____ 1. Algeria peacefully gained its independence from France.

_____ 2. Most Third World countries used to be colonies of other nations.

_____ 3. John Paul II was the first Italian pope in one thousand years.

_____ 4. John Paul II asked for his would-be assassin to be released from prison.

_____ 5. Communism suffered a series of defeats around the world after John Paul II consecrated the world to Mary.

_____ 6. The Cold War ended with the collapse of the Soviet Union.

_____ 7. The Communists agreed with Pope John Paul on most subjects.

_____ 8. The fall of Communism was bloodless and peaceful all over Europe.

_____ 9. East and West Berlin were reunited after the fall of the Berlin Wall.

____ 10. John Paul II's teachings helped bring about the fall of Communism.

CHAPTER 35
An Uncertain Future

Perfect Score: 100   Your Score: _____

True or False?

Directions: In the blank beside each statement, write "T" if the statement is *True* or "F" if the statement is *False*. Each correct answer is worth 10 points. 50 possible points.

_____ 1. Pope John Paul II's Feast Day is October 22.

_____ 2. The countries of the European Union share common laws and a common currency.

_____ 3. European parents are having more and more children.

_____ 4. John Paul II published a new *Catechism of the Catholic Church*.

_____ 5. After the fall of Communism, there was no more fighting anywhere in Europe.

Multiple Choice

Directions: For each numbered item, circle the letter beside the choice (A, B, C, or D) that best answers the question or completes the statement. Circle only one choice per item. Each correct answer is worth 10 points. 50 possible points.

1. Members of the European Union use _____ for currency.

A. pesos
B. dollars
C. euros
D. change

2. Some churches in Europe have been converted into:

A. museums.
B. mosques.
C. government buildings.
D. affordable housing.

3. John Paul II reigned as pope for:

A. twelve years.
B. three years.
C. seventy-eight years.
D. twenty-seven years.

4. Many non-European immigrants who come to Europe are:

A. Muslim.
B. Greek Orthodox.
C. Jewish.
D. American.

5. Christendom:

A. exists in Europe today.
B. fell apart because of sin and the failures of men.
C. migrated with Puritans to the Americas.
D. was destroyed by Muslims.

ANSWER KEY

CHAPTER 1—The Glory of the Renaissance
Test Book pages 1–4

Multiple Choice
1. B   2. C   3. A   4. A   5. D   6. B   7. D   8. D   9. C   10. A

True or False?
1. T   2. T   3. F   4. T   5. F   6. T   7. T   8. F   9. T   10. T

CHAPTER 2—Columbus and the New World
Test Book pages 5–6

Matching
1. C   2. G   3. I   4. E   5. A   6. H   7. B   8. D   9. F   10. J

CHAPTER 3—Martin Luther
Test Book pages 7–8

True or False?
1. T   2. T   3. F   4. T   5. T   6. F   7. F   8. T   9. F   10. T   11. T   12. T
13. F   14. T   15. F   16. T   17. T   18. F   19. T   20. T

CHAPTER 4—Germany on Fire
Test Book pages 9–10

Multiple Choice
1. C   2. D   3. C   4. A   5. D   6. C   7. B   8. A   9. B   10. D

CHAPTER 5—Henry VIII and Anglicanism
Test Book pages 11–14

Matching
1. I   2. A   3. C   4. F   5. J   6. D   7. B   8. G   9. E   10. H

Multiple Choice
1. B   2. D   3. A   4. C   5. C   6. D   7. D   8. A   9. C   10. B

CHAPTER 6—The French Wars of Religion
Test Book pages 15–18

True or False?
1. T   2. F   3. T   4. T   5. F   6. T   7. F   8. T   9. F   10. F

Multiple Choice
1. B   2. A   3. C   4. C   5. B   6. A   7. D   8. A   9. B   10. D

CHAPTER 7—Mary, Queen of Scots
Test Book pages 19–20

Multiple Choice
1. C   2. A   3. B   4. C   5. A   6. B   7. C   8. B   9. D   10. C

CHAPTER 8—The Counter-Reformation
Test Book pages 21–24

Matching
1. B   2. F   3. C   4. E   5. A   6. G   7. D   8. J   9. H   10. I

Multiple Choice
1. A   2. D   3. B   4. C   5. B   6. D   7. C   8. B   9. A   10. C

CHAPTER 9—Pope St. Pius V and the Battle of Lepanto
Test Book pages 25–26

True or False?
1. F 2. T 3. T 4. F 5. T 6. F 7. T 8. F 9. T 10. T

CHAPTER 10—The Age of Elizabeth
Test Book pages 27–30

Multiple Choice
1. B 2. A 3. C 4. D 5. D 6. A 7. C 8. D 9. C 10. A

True or False?
1. F 2. T 3. T 4. F 5. T 6. F 7. T 8. T 9. T 10. F

CHAPTER 11—King Philip II
Test Book pages 31–32

Multiple Choice
1. D 2. A 3. B 4. B 5. A

Matching
1. G 2. H 3. A 4. O 5. I 6. B 7. J 8. D 9. N 10. F 11. L 12. C
13. K 14. M 15. E

CHAPTER 12—The Thirty Years' War
Test Book pages 33–34

Multiple Choice
1. D 2. C 3. D 4. B 5. D 6. B 7. C 8. B 9. A 10. B

CHAPTER 13—Roundheads and Cavaliers
Test Book pages 35–38

True or False?
1. T   2. T   3. F   4. F   5. T   6. F   7. T   8. F   9. T   10. F

Multiple Choice
1. A   2. C   3. B   4. B   5. D   6. A   7. D   8. D   9. C   10. B

CHAPTER 14—The Restoration and the Not-So-Glorious Revolution
Test Book pages 39–40

Matching
1. J   2. C   3. G   4. E   5. H   6. I   7. F   8. B   9. D   10. A

CHAPTER 15—The Age of the Sun King
Test Book pages 41–44

Multiple Choice
1. D   2. B   3. D   4. A   5. C   6. B   7. D   8. B   9. A   10. D   11. C   12. B
13. B   14. A   15. C   16. B

True or False?
1. F   2. T   3. T   4. F

CHAPTER 16—The Turkish Threat
Test Book pages 45–47

Matching
1. F   2. T   3. L   4. N   5. B   6. S   7. D   8. C   9. J   10. P   11. R   12. H
13. I   14. Q   15. A   16. G   17. K   18. E   19. O   20. M

CHAPTER 17—The Jacobites
Test Book pages 47–48

True or False?
1. T   2. T   3. F   4. F   5. T   6. F   7. T   8. T   9. T   10. F

CHAPTER 18—Light and Darkness
Test Book pages 49–52

Multiple Choice
1. C   2. B   3. D   4. A   5. A   6. C   7. C   8. A   9. B   10. D   11. D   12. B
13. D   14. C   15. B   16. A   17. C   18. B   19. C   20. D

CHAPTER 19—A World at War
Test Book pages 53–54

Matching
1. C   2. H   3. J   4. D   5. A   6. E   7. I   8. F   9. G   10. B

True or False?
1. F   2. T   3. T   4. F   5. T   6. T   7. F   8. T   9. T   10. T

CHAPTER 20—The French Revolution
Test Book pages 55–56

Multiple Choice
1. D   2. C   3. D   4. D   5. D   6. C   7. A   8. B   9. B   10. D

CHAPTER 21—The Rise and Fall of Napoleon
Test Book pages 57–58

Matching
1. S   2. J   3. E   4. D   5. O   6. H   7. G   8. Q   9. T   10. N   11. A   12. C
13. F   14. I   15. R   16. K   17. P   18. M   19. B   20. L

CHAPTER 22—Peace Returns
Test Book pages 59–60

Multiple Choice
1. B   2. C   3. D   4. A   5. D   6. A   7. D   8. C   9. B   10. D

CHAPTER 23—Reforms and Revolutions
Test Book pages 61–62

True or False?
1. T   2. T   3. F   4. T   5. F   6. T   7. F   8. T   9. F   10. T

CHAPTER 24—The Unification of Italy and Germany
Test Book pages 63–66

Multiple Choice
1. D   2. C   3. A   4. B   5. C

True or False?
1. F   2. F   3. T   4. T   5. T

Matching
1. C   2. H   3. I   4. J   5. A   6. D   7. E   8. B   9. F   10. G

CHAPTER 25—The Popes Against the World
Test Book pages 67–68

True or False?
1. F   2. T   3. T   4. F   5. F   6. T   7. T   8. T   9. F   10. T

Matching
1. C   2. H   3. B   4. J   5. D   6. F   7. E   8. A   9. I   10. G

CHAPTER 26—Europe Conquers the Globe
Test Book pages 69–70

Multiple Choice
1. C   2. D   3. C   4. A   5. D

Matching
1. B   2. E   3. C   4. A   5. D

CHAPTER 27—The Great War
Test Book pages 71–72

True or False?
1. F   2. T   3. T   4. F   5. T   6. F   7. T   8. F   9. T   10. F

Matching
1. B   2. G   3. J   4. C   5. E   6. F   7. A   8. H   9. D   10. I

CHAPTER 28—The Rise of the Dictators
Test Book pages 73–74

Multiple Choice
1. C   2. D   3. A   4. B   5. C

True or False?
1. T   2. F   3. T   4. T   5. F

Matching
1. C   2. G   3. I   4. A   5. H   6. D   7. J   8. B   9. E   10. F

CHAPTER 29—The Second World War
Test Book pages 75–76

Matching
1. D   2. G   3. H   4. C   5. I   6. A   7. J   8. E   9. B   10. F

CHAPTER 30—The Third Reich Collapses
Test Book pages 77–78

Multiple Choice
1. A   2. C   3. B   4. C   5. D

True or False?
1. T   2. F   3. T   4. T   5. T

Matching
1. J   2. B   3. G   4. H   5. A   6. E   7. D   8. F   9. I   10. C

CHAPTER 31—The Cold War
Test Book pages 79–82

Multiple Choice
1. B   2. C   3. B   4. D   5. C

True or False?
1. T   2. F   3. T   4. F   5. T

Matching
1. C   2. E   3. H   4. A   5. J   6. D   7. F   8. B   9. I   10. G

CHAPTER 32—Changes in the Modern World
Test Book pages 83–84

Matching
1. C   2. A   3. E   4. B   5. D

True or False?
1. F   2. T   3. T   4. T   5. F

CHAPTER 33—The Second Vatican Council
Test Book pages 85–88

Multiple Choice
1. A   2. C   3. B   4. C   5. B

True or False?
1. T   2. T   3. T   4. T   5. F   6. T   7. F   8. T   9. F   10. F

Matching
1. C   2. B   3. D   4. A   5. E

CHAPTER 34—The End of the Cold War
Test Book pages 89–90

Matching
1. F   2. D   3. A   4. H   5. E   6. B   7. J   8. C   9. I   10. G

True or False?
1. F   2. T   3. F   4. T   5. T   6. T   7. F   8. F   9. T   10. T

CHAPTER 35—An Uncertain Future
Test Book pages 91–92

True or False?
1. T   2. T   3. F   4. T   5. F

Multiple Choice
1. C   2. B   3. D   4. A   5. B